P🐾SiTiVeLY GeORgia'S

Guide to Surviving Grief

Elizabeth Ferris

Hasmark
PUBLISHING
INTERNATIONAL

Illustrations: Matrix Solutions

Editor: Allison Burney
allison@hasmarkpublishing.com

Book Design: Anne Karklins
anne@hasmarkpublishing.com

ISBN 13: 978-1-989756-46-1
ISBN 10: 1989756468

The loss of a loved one is a gut-wrenching experience. How do you overcome it?

Hello, my name is Positively Georgia. I am a motivational Airedale Terrier dog. I'm 10 years old and I would like to help you. I think of myself as a unique therapy dog. I want to be of service to humans all over the world. I currently live in Northwestern Canada with my owner, Norman. I am the company mascot and I get to go to work with my Norman every day. I listen a lot as we drive around to various places. I also have a unique talent of smelling emotions. My sniffing sense is so powerful that I can sniff what people are feeling. I like that you sniffed out this book today. Thank you for leading with your nose like me.

My days are pretty amazing. I get to travel around with my owner Norman in his big black truck. My Norman helps people buy and sell their houses. Some days, though, I can sniff out sadness. I can tell that some people are selling because a family member has passed away. They are attempting to move on even though they are in pain. This pain shows on their faces and especially in their eyes. Other times, a family pet has passed away, and it's very sad for them to look at the spot in the house where that pet once laid and played. I understand love. Love for another soul is an amazing, powerful gift. I love my Norman very much and I never leave his side. We are buddies for life, and I would do anything to protect him and bring joy to his days. He says I'm a good dog. I like it when he pats my head and tells me this. I am a proud Airedale.

Thank you for deciding to pick up this book today and read my Georgia thoughts. Since you are suffering from such a terrible loss of a loved one or pet, you must be in a low-energy place. My hope is to help you get moving forward, however hard that may seem at this time. I am here to remind you that you have all the power you need within you. Feel it strengthening your body with every thought. You can and will overcome this. I believe in you.

I've watched sadness take over a human before. Several years ago, I was witness to a mother who lost her grown son unexpectedly. This is when I first realized I am a unique therapy dog. I spent many nights during those early days jumping up onto the couch and squishing her with my big furry body in hopes of cheering her up. I'd squish her so hard sometimes that she would giggle and say, 'Why Georgia, why?" It's fun for me to throw my weight around. I once heard someone say, "If you've got it, flaunt it." I like to flaunt my big-boned frame wherever and however I can.

Other times, in the middle of the night I would sneak into her bedroom. I'd tap her bed with my paw, wake her up and lick her nose, just to make sure she knew I had a watchful eye over her. When she went to the bathroom, I'd stand guard. My duty was to protect her and remind her that I'm always there watching. Sometimes I was so good at sneaking up on her and watching her that she didn't even see me! A couple of times, she accidentally stepped on my paw and almost tripped. My bad! I'm sure there are watchful eyes around you as well. Perhaps they are across the room right now, looking at you as you read this. Maybe they are watching from heaven or a special spiritual place. Either way, you will be okay. Someone is always close to you who truly does care about you and is protecting you.

It is okay to be sad and to remember your loved one. It is okay to think of them and keep their memory alive. You love them with all your heart. You will always love and miss them; this we know to be true. The pain of losing them will always be there, but my hope for you is that you will be able to learn to redirect that pain into a positive vibration. That will, in turn, help you become strong and healthy. I often hear my owner Norman say to people, "You can't get sick enough to bring someone back." I think that is so important, and I want you to read it again: "You can't get sick enough to bring someone back." My hope for you is that you realize you must be healthy. You have to be – people love and care for you and need you.

From what I know about love, I believe that we are still connected to our loved ones even if we can no longer see them. We are able to bring back good thoughts and memories of our loved ones at any time. Those memories will never be taken away. The memories of time spent together and the love and laughter shared is truly a most prized gift. Be grateful for that time together. I'm grateful for all the good memories I have of the creatures and humans within my world and heart.

I often hear my owner say, "Life is for the living. The tragedy didn't happen to you; it happened to them." It took me a couple of years to figure that out, but now I understand. You can be sad for the loss of your loved one, but don't let the tragedy continue to spill into your present life to the point where your life is not one of joy and hope anymore. As you know, life truly goes by fast. It goes by fast even when you pay attention. Life goes by especially fast for me. They tell me that in dog years, I'm seventy. How is that possible? Does that mean my furry body had seventy birthday parties? If so, where are all the extra birthday doggy treats? Also, bring bacon to my party. I like bacon. If time is going to fly by so fast, wouldn't you want to see yourself smiling when you look back at your memories? I would. You have a great smile! Don't forget that. Is that bacon I see in your teeth? Nice!

I think the first step to helping you move forward is to really activate your imagination, like I do when I'm travelling around with my Norman. You can start by visualizing that your loved one is still here, but is on vacation or too busy to call or connect with you. This will help you get through the early days. Your brain will stop focusing on the tragedy and you'll be able to at least have a chance to focus on other things, no matter how small they may be.

Now you need to focus. Step out of the fog within your head. Get your butt out of bed and shower or have a bath every day. This is mandatory – no matter what. Set your alarm and just get the heck up! It doesn't do anybody any good to spend your amazing life buried deep within a pillow of sadness. The water will help sooth your mind, body and soul. Feel its healing powers flow over you. Be grateful for this gift of water and how it makes you feel. I always feel so much better after my Norman takes me for a swim in the river by his work. It's refreshing and exhilarating. I highly recommend water to cleanse your soul (and, of course, get rid of stinky dog armpit smells!) I can't smell myself, but my Norman sometimes says, "Phew, Georgia! You are a stinky dog!" I think that's just him farting, but it's okay. I'll pretend I don't notice..

Now smile. Fake it if you must, but smile. Give yourself permission to feel positive. If your loved one is able to check up on you from heaven, make them proud and let them know you are okay and are moving forward. You can do this! We believe in you. SMILE!

Now it's time to act. Put away your loved one's items as soon as possible. Resist the urge to smell their clothes or stare at their photos. Once you have had time to deal with the pain, it is okay to bring out some memorabilia, but don't do this too soon. I know you think you will only spend a couple of moments reliving memories shared, but you might just fall further and further down the rabbit hole. We want you getting better and moving forward! Resist the urge to look in the rear view mirror for now. I've ventured down a couple of rabbit holes in my past, and I realize now that it was not only unhelpful – it made me stink like digested carrots! Don't be a stinky carrot like me!.

Now live. Open your eyes and really look at the people who are around you. Really take the time to see them. They are willing you to keep going. Feel their energy strengthening you with every breath you take and every glance received. These could be direct family members, strangers, and even those who pass by you on the street. We are all connected to this amazing source of energy and you can pull from it to heal your sadness. Your body is made to heal itself. You will get through this. You are strong. I like to make people look at me. I bark a lot and enjoy drawing lots of attention to myself. Don't make me bark at you! My bark sounds like I'm a big, tough dog, but I'm really just saying, "Hi! Great to see you! Have a wonderful day!"

26

Now think and be grateful. Think of the sunshine. Feel its bright rays bringing energy and hope to your body once again. This is a gift from your soul. Every time you look to the bright blue sky and see the beautiful white fluffy clouds moving, remember to be thankful for this day. The sun is your healing light. Be grateful and find joy in every day. You can do it! I like to lay on the green grass in front of our house. I lay on my back and stick my four paws up into the sky. I like to pretend I'm giving the clouds a high-five for the awesome job they are doing, just by being them. High-five to you, too! Look at you, continuing onwards by reading this book and letting your imagination step into the world of my Georgia thoughts. Feel better? I hope you do.

On my travels throughout the day with my Norman, I often hear people say they are too busy for this or that. They don't have enough time for anything. Or something sad has happened, and they feel as if they just can't cope anymore, so they shut down. I like to make a list in my head. I start by thinking about what, exactly, I want to accomplish today. The lists in my head always start with, "Bark at five or more people." I check that off consistently. Start writing down goals for what you want to accomplish each day. Make a list. It doesn't matter whether they are small goals, like getting out of bed, bathing, and eating breakfast, or bigger goals like helping others and sharing what you have learned. Write them down. Then check them off your list and continue to move onwards and upwards, one step at a time. This is how I keep my paws going; one step at a time. Sometimes I get so excited about the thought of helping others, I run around the yard so fast that my back two paws barely touch the ground! I'm a pretty big-boned Airedale, but I try to make myself look very graceful – even when I run so hard I slide into my own front paws! .

Besides my sniffer, one of my other gifts is that I have exceptional hearing. I think the quickest way to feel better and happier is to bring delight to your ears and play upbeat music. Try it! Play some upbeat, happy music. Do not watch sad movies or take part in sad conversations. You are above that, and will only speak positively from this moment forward! You have had enough of being sad; this is your time to bring your emotions up. Think of me, Positively Georgia, shaking my booty to a catchy song. Why yes, yes indeed, I do have rhythm! Want to dance with me?

Remember what you love, and be grateful for all you have. Make a list of five or more things that bring you joy. I am grateful for my positive attitude, the ability to help others, bacon snacks, my Norman, swimming in the river, and my big-boned frame that makes me stand out. Once you have completed your list, really look at everything you are grateful for. See how truly lucky you are? Don't forget that. You are worthy of all those things, experiences and love. You are absolutely amazing! Never forget how strong you are. You will get through anything because your soul is telling you to press on.

JOY

GRATITUDE

BALANCE

LOVE

HARMONY

PEACE

Stay focused on positive thoughts. This is your life. Take the time to be good to yourself. Spread your peace, love, joy and gratitude out into the universe. Also, if you see me riding around in my Norman's truck, please bring me bacon snacks!.

The eND.

About the Author

Georgia Ferris is a bright-eyed and furry tailed Airedale Terrier with a very positive outlook on life. Georgia lives with her humans, Norman and Elizabeth, in Western Canada. When Georgia is not daydreaming of bacon snacks, she continues to write endearing stores, of inspiration and positive values to help teen and young adults realize their amazing potential. She still loves shaking her booty to a catchy song.

www.ferrisbooks.com

More books in the
POSiTiveLY GeORgia Series

Georgia is a bright-eyed and furry tailed Airedale Terrier with a very positive outlook on life.

POSiTiveLY GeORgia will inspire you to dream and challenge you to remember your unique potential. It will encourage you to focus your good energy and create great things. Share your gifts with the world like Georgia. This book was created to bring positive thoughts to children (and parents) of all ages!

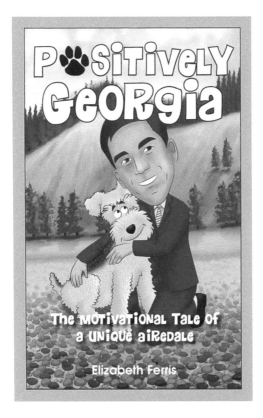

Giving a Voice to Creativity!

With every donation, a voice will be given to the creativity that lies within the hearts of our children living with diverse challenges.

By making this difference, children that may not have been given the opportunity to have their Heart Heard will have the freedom to create beautiful works of art and musical creations.

Donate by visiting

HeartstobeHeard.com

We thank you.

CPSIA information can be obtained
at www.ICGtesting.com
Printed in the USA
BVHW021346240720
584441BV00006B/113